The **BOOK** of **me!**

Adam Frost

BLOOMSBURY
LONDON OXFORD NEW YORK NEW DELHI SYDNEY

illustrated by
Sarah Ray

To Anna and Eliza

Bloomsbury Children's Books
An imprint of Bloomsbury Publishing Plc
50 Bedford Square London WC1B 3DP UK

www.bloomsbury.com

BLOOMSBURY and the Diana logo are trademarks
of Bloomsbury Publishing Plc

Published in Great Britain 2017

A catalogue record for this book is available from the British Library.

Library of Congress Cataloguing-in-Publication data has been applied for.

ISBN: 9781408876817

2 4 6 8 10 9 7 5 3 1

Printed and bound in Great Britain by CPI Group (UK) Ltd, Croydon CR0 4YY

MIX
Paper from
responsible sources
FSC
www.fsc.org   FSC® C020471

This book is produced using paper that is made from wood grown in managed, sustainable forests. It is natural, renewable and recyclable. The logging and manufacturing processes conform to the environmental regulations of the country of origin.

To find out more about our authors and books visit www.bloomsbury.com. Here you will find extracts, author interviews, details of forthcoming events and the option to sign up for our newsletters.

THIS IS ME

My first name is:_____

Middle name:_____

Surname:_____

Nicknames:_____

_____

_____

If you don't have one, just make one up!

DID YOU KNOW?

You have to have a name. Your parents have six weeks after your birth to register your name. Or they're

BREAKING THE LAW.

oops

CALL ME SPIDERMAN

Did you know that when you're an adult you can change your name? It's called making a deed poll. Here are five unusual name changes.

Born: JOHN DENTON

↓

New name: WILLY WONKA

Born: AVA PAYNE

↓

New name: AVA TRULY SCRUMPTIOUS

Born: CHARLOTTE PRICE

New name: PINK SPARKLY AND ALL THINGS NICE

Born: DAVID LENNOX

↓

New name: HER MAJESTY THE QUEEN

But perhaps the craziest is...

Born: DANIEL KNOX-HEWSON

↓

New name: EMPEROR SPIDERMAN GANDALF WOLVERINE SKYWALKER OPTIMUS PRIME GOKU SONIC XAVIER RYU CLOUD SUPERMAN HEMAN BATMAN THRASH

If you changed your name, what would you change it to?

_____

_____

MY NAME IS

?

I LIVE HERE...

Put a cross where you live on this map:

How about this map?

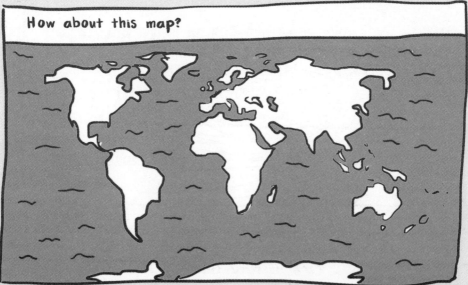

Put a cross where you live on this map too!

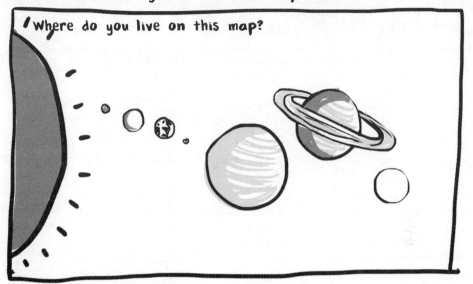

Where do you live on this map?

What about this map?

This one's tricky... Turn over to find out the answer.

OUR HOME GALAXY

You live here

Write your favourite facts about the Milky Way here.
There are some example facts over there ———> to help you.

~~~~~~

~~~~~~

~~~~~~

Draw a friendly alien here.

Draw a scary alien here.

The Earth is located in the Orion Spur region of the Milky Way.

Earth is about 25,000 light years from the centre of the galaxy.

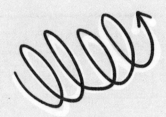

We're constantly spinning round the edge of the Milky Way. It takes us about 250 million years to go round once.

The Milky Way and its neighbour Andromeda are flying towards each other at 270,000 mph. In about 4 billion years, they'll collide.

BANG!

HOME SWEET HOME

Which type of building do you live in?
Tick one of the options below — or draw your own.

☐ House

☐ Cottage

☐ Flat or apartment

☐ Bungalow

☐ Treehouse

☐ Igloo

☐ Cave

☐ Castle

☐ Houseboat

☐ Yurt

Did we miss yours out? Draw it here. ↘

BIZARRE BUILDINGS

Fancy living in one of these GENUINE places?

1.

In Krasnoyarsk, Russia, there is a house built upside down.

2.

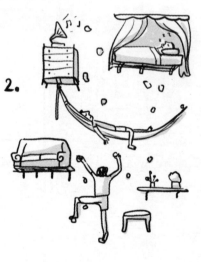

In Rio, Brazil, Tiago and Gabriel Primo built a 'vertical house' on a climbing wall, tying hammocks to the footholds.

3.

Pierre André Senizerques has built a skateboard house, with ramps on every wall.

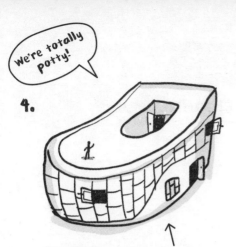

4.

In Korea, there is a house shaped like a giant toilet.

5.

In Oxford, UK, there is a house with a huge fibreglass shark sticking out of a hole in the roof. It's been there for 30 years.

6.

In Japan, there is a completely see-through house. The roof and all the walls are made of glass!

I'd like to live in

☐ House 1	☐ House 4		
☐ House 2	☐ House 5	☐ None of these houses. They're all bonkers!
☐ House 3	☐ House 6		

MY ROOM

Have you got a sign on your door?
Design your own room sign.

Some ideas over there...

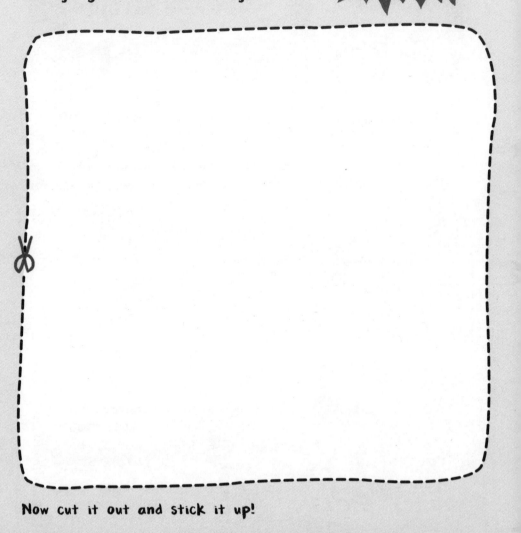

Now cut it out and stick it up!

WHAT'S THE PASSWORD?

Write down a password to get into your room.

Now rip out this page, screw it into a ball and SWALLOW IT!★

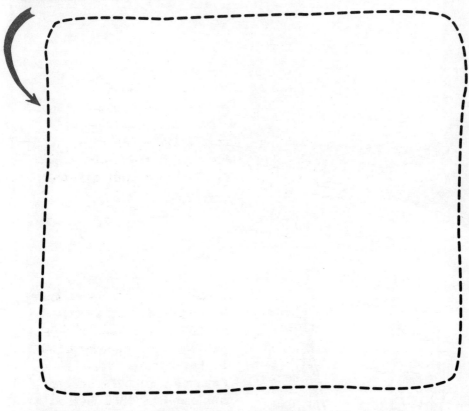

★Swallowing paper is a bit disgusting. So maybe:

i) put some salt on it first
ii) just throw it in the bin instead.
Paper has WEIRD chemicals in it.

The most common computer password is '123456'. The second most common is 'password'.

The most famous password in the world is 'Open sesame'. It is used in the story 'Ali Baba and the Forty Thieves' to open a cave full of gold.

Flash

thunder

Sometimes, when you give a password, the other person ALSO has to give a password (a 'countersign'). In the Second World War, American soldiers greeted any soldiers they met with the word 'flash'. The other soldier had to say 'thunder' to prove they were a friend.

MY DREAM ROOM

Draw your perfect bedroom here.

What would it look like? What would be inside?
We've put some ideas on the opposite page.

A slide that leads to the garden

A fireman's pole to take you down to the living room

A pit covered with branches to catch your brother when he sneaks in to take your stuff

grgh!

A hover bed

A door with a sliding panel in so you can open it and demand a password

A wardrobe that leads to Narnia

19

CIRCLE ANY FOOD YOU LIKE

Cheese

Hamburger

Peas

Carrots

Apple

Banana

Sweets

Orange

Chicken

Spaghetti

Chips

Chocolate

Ice cream

Sweetcorn

Onion

Bacon

Lemon

Crisps

Bread

Mushrooms

Rice

Sausage

Fish

Tomatoes

Coconut

Prawn

Broccoli

Pepper

Cereal

Pear

Pretzel

Jam

Lollipop

Strawberries

Cherries

20 Soup

Tea

Pancake

Chilli

PUT A CROSS THROUGH ANY YOU DON'T

Noodles

Pineapple

Beans

Yoghurt

Milk

Olives

Pumpkin

Hot dog

Cupcake

Peanuts

Boiled Egg

Porridge

Grapes

Ketchup

Birthday cake

Pie

Fried egg

Baguette

Pizza

Celery

Biscuits

Croissant

Popcorn

Ham sandwich

Did we miss out any of your favourite food? Draw it here.

ANYBODY HOME?

Who else lives in your house? Draw them here.

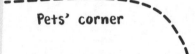

Pets' corner

OH BROTHER!

If you've got a brother or sister, tick
if any of these have ever happened.

YES   NO

 They did something wrong
and told my parents it was
me □ □

 They gave me an annoying
nickname □ □

 They stole some of my
crisps or sweets □ □

 They drew on my
desk/wall/arms □ □

 They tried to persuade
my parents to 'take
me back to the shop' □ □

 They tried to sell my
stuff on the internet □ □

Did you know? Brothers and sisters fight
(on average) between THREE and
FOUR times AN HOUR.

23

MY MUM

(Or cross out 'Mum' and put Nan, Gran, Aunt or whoever you like!)

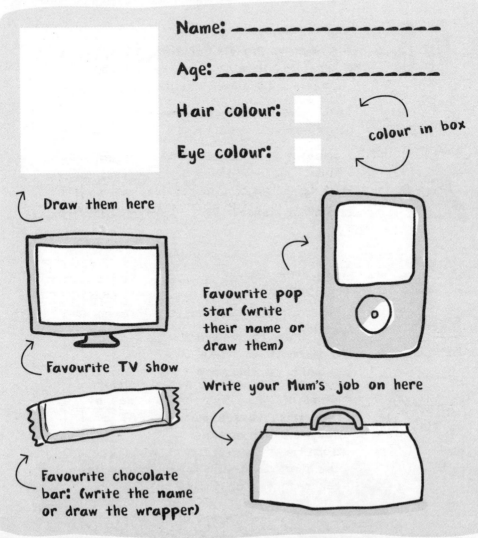

Name: —————————————————

Age: —————————————————

Hair colour: [ ]

Eye colour: [ ]

colour in box

Draw them here

Favourite pop star (write their name or draw them)

Favourite TV show

Write your Mum's job on here

Favourite chocolate bar: (write the name or draw the wrapper)

WORLD'S WORST MUMS

Does your Mum get on your nerves? Bet she's an angel compared to these real-life mothers!

A mum in South Carolina, USA, had her 12-year-old-son arrested for opening his Christmas presents early.

Imagine if Annalisa Flanagan was your Mum. She has the world's loudest voice! At 121 decibels, it's as loud as a jet engine. GET UP FOR SCHOOL - NOW!!

Jenny Chapman's kids have to put up with the world's loudest snore. At 112 decibels, you can hear it through two walls.

But at least you're not a hamster. Hamster mums have an average of nine pups, but sometimes EAT a couple of them.
Sometimes this happens when one of the pups is crying loudly and putting the rest of the family in danger.

RUN!

SO EMBARRASSING!

Mums really know how to embarrass you.
Award yourself 10 POINTS for any of the things
below that your Mum has done.

Shown baby photos
to my friends

Given me a sloppy
kiss at the school
games

Tidied my room so I
can't find anything

Told my friends an
embarrassing story
about something I did
when I was little

 Brushed my hair so hard it made my eyes water

Asked me how their own mobile phone works

 Bought me clothes that I will never wear in a million years

Bye now Timmypoo! Called me a babyish name in front of my friends

20 POINT BONUS FOR:

Spat on a hanky or tissue and then wiped something off my face

Now work out your total score. →

Scores:

0-30 points

Hurrah! Your Mum is cool!

40-70 points

Your Mum is pretty embarrassing. Could be worse though. She could be as embarrassing as DAD.

80-100 points

NOOO! Every time your Mum does anything, you feel like CURLING UP INTO A BALL!

REMEMBER

You can always take your revenge by embarrassing your mum instead. Try practicing one of the incredible skills on page 42.

NO MORE CHORES!

The next time your parents ask you to help around the house, show them this simple price list.

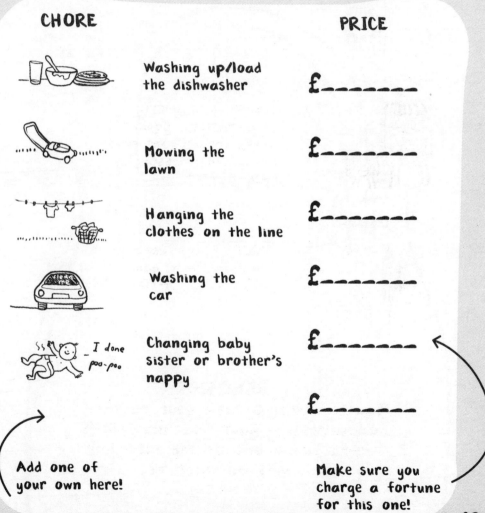

CHORE	PRICE
Washing up/load the dishwasher	£_____
Mowing the lawn	£_____
Hanging the clothes on the line	£_____
Washing the car	£_____
Changing baby sister or brother's nappy	£_____
	£_____

Add one of your own here!

Make sure you charge a fortune for this one!

IT'S IN THE BAG!

We all know Mum's handbag is like Dr Who's TARDIS. What's she got in there? Draw your best guess at the contents here.

Some ideas for what you could draw.

Purse

Lipstick

Tissues

Pen

Small dog

First aid

Mobile phone

Emergency chocolate bar

Really small mirror

Some fluff

A book

Umbrella

Hairbrush

A diary

Sunglasses

Photo wallet containing lovely pictures of you

Hairpins and clips

Business card

Gloves

Phone charger

Needle and thread

Library card

Keys

Stamps

WEIGH TO GO

Mums' handbags can weigh a ton. Put your Mum's on the bathroom scales and see how it measures up.

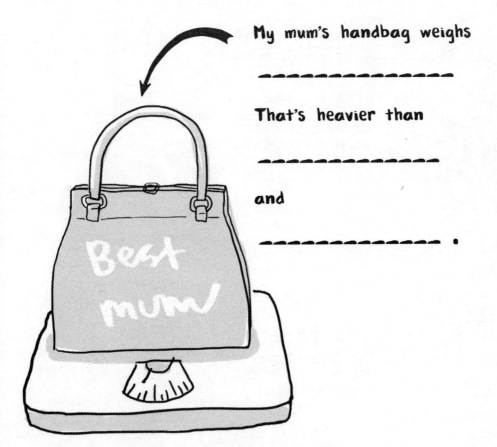

My mum's handbag weighs

————————————

That's heavier than

————————————

and

————————————.

Here are some objects you can use for comparison.

gerbil 40g

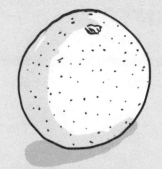

grapefruit 130g

can of fizzy
drink 366g

brick 2,500g

newborn baby 3,400g

bowling ball 5,000g

baby elephant 91,000g

FANCY PANTS

Design a pair of lucky pants (or knickers!).

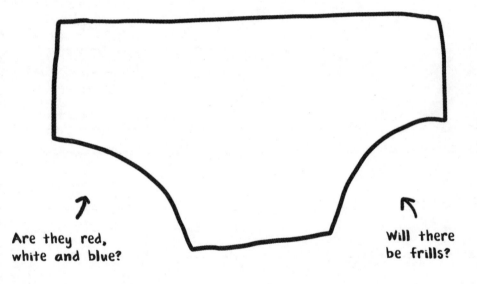

Are they red,
white and blue?

Will there
be frills?

Cover them with your favourite things.

LEFT RIGHT LEFT RIGHT

How good are you at writing with your OTHER hand? Could you be AMBIDEXTROUS?

	LEFT HAND	RIGHT HAND
Write your name	_____	_____
Write your street name	_____ _____	_____ _____
Write your best friend's name	_____ _____	_____ _____
Write the name of your favourite animal	_____ _____ _____	_____ _____ _____
Write the title of your favourite song	_____ _____ _____	_____ _____ _____

HOW OLD AM I?

Right NOW, I am...

_____ years

_____ months

_____ weeks

_____ days

_____ hours

_____ minutes

and   _____ seconds OLD.

In DOG YEARS, I am ___ years old.
(Multiply your age by SEVEN).

In GUINEA PIG YEARS, I am ___ years old.
(Multiply your age by SIXTEEN).

In MOUSE YEARS, I am ___ years old.
(Multiply your age by FORTY).

In ROBIN YEARS, I am ___ years old.
(Multiply your age by SEVENTY).

In ELEPHANT YEARS, I am ___ years old.
(Multiply your age by ONE).★

★An elephant's lifespan is the same as ours!

ROLL WITH IT

Which of the following can you do?★

FORWARD ROLL Difficulty level: Easy

☐ I can do this!

BACKWARD ROLL Difficulty level: Easy

☐ Nailed it!

HEADSTAND Difficulty level: Medium

☐ Achievement unlocked!

★When throwing yourself around, make sure you are somewhere safe where you won't break yourself and anything else. And ask an adult first!

CARTWHEEL Difficulty level: Quite Hard

☐ I can do this!

THE SPLITS Difficulty level: Quite Hard

☐ Nailed it!

BACKFLIP Difficulty level: Very Hard

☐ I'm born to do it!

Can you walk on your hands?

How far? _____ metres

AMAZING ACROBATS

1. Sarah Chapman from Glastonbury, UK walked five kilometres on her hands in 2002. It took her eight hours.

2. In 2012, Ziyi Zhang did **36** backflips in **ONE MINUTE.**

3. In 2010, Abhinandan Sadalge, a nine-year-old boy from India performed **1,321** cartwheels in a row. It took him **37 minutes and 53 seconds.**

4. Zlata is the world's most flexible woman. She can fit inside a 50 square centimetre box.

175cm

50cm

PAPER POWER!

Remember, read the other side before you start ripping!

Rip out this page. Then try to fold it **SEVEN TIMES**.

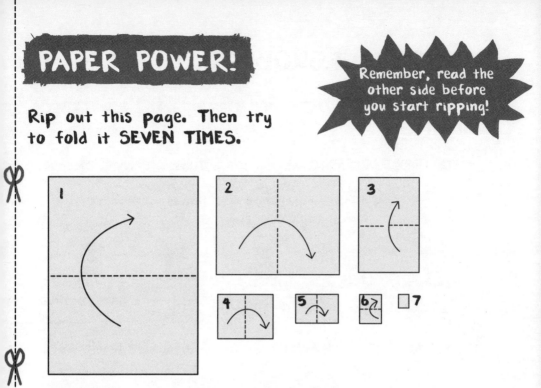

Until 2002, it was believed you could only fold paper a maximum of **SEVEN TIMES** but...

In 2002 Britney Gallivan folded a roll of toilet paper twelve times.

In 2012, students from St Mark's School, Southborough managed thirteen folds.

SUPERSKILLS

Forget acrobatics! These are the only skills worth having...

THE UNDERARM FART   Difficulty level: Medium

☐ I can do this!

BURPING THE ALPHABET   Difficulty level: Hard

☐ Nailed it!

BALANCING SPOON ON NOSE   Difficulty level: Medium

☐ Achievement unlocked

I can also:

Tick the box if you've mastered the skill

Click my fingers ☐

Cross my eyes ☐

Wolf whistle ☐

Blow a bubble as big as my face ☐

Do a Vulcan salute ☐

Raise one eyebrow ☐

MY BABY TEETH

Shade any wobbly teeth GREY. If any have fallen out, colour them in BLACK.

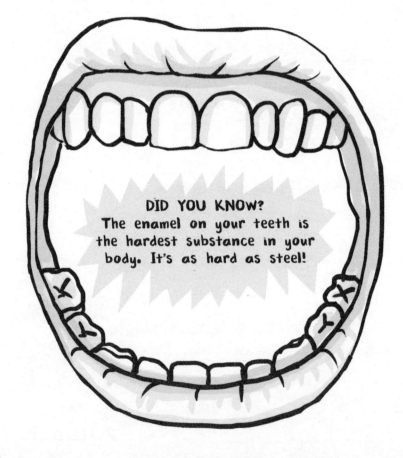

DID YOU KNOW?
The enamel on your teeth is the hardest substance in your body. It's as hard as steel!

Total number of grown-up teeth:

Write this as a tally chart so you can keep adding to it.

(this is a tally chart)

You will get between 28 and 32 ADULT TEETH.

WHAT'S IT WORTH?

Keep track of what the Tooth Fairy has given you.

You're welcome!

1._____   8._____   15._____
2._____   9._____   16._____
3._____   10._____   17._____
4._____   11._____   18._____
5._____   12._____   19._____
6._____   13._____   20._____
7._____   14._____

Total £_____

TOP OF THE CHOPPERS

How do you measure up to our animal friends?

A narwhal has two teeth.

You have up to 32 teeth.

A snail has around 14,000 teeth.

A dolphin only gets one set of teeth in its lifetime.

You will have two sets of teeth: baby teeth and grown-up teeth.

A shark gets a new set every two weeks and has HUNDREDS of sets in its lifetime.

Draw a monster with the scariest teeth in the world here!

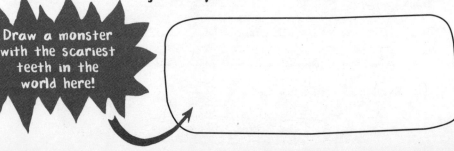

A coypu or river rat has orange teeth.

You have white teeth.

A sea otter often has purple teeth.

eating a purple sea urchin

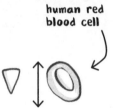

human red blood cell

2.5cm

a stamp

a-four year-old child

A bedbug's teeth are a few micrometres.

Your longest adult tooth will be about 2.5 centimetres.

A walrus's tusk can be one metre long.

BITE this (that will use your INCISORS)

TEAR it out (that uses your CANINES)

CHEW it (that will use your MOLARS)

But DON'T swallow it (humans can't digest paper).

DO YOU SCREAM FOR ICE CREAM?

Colour these in so they look like your favourite flavours.

Add sprinkles, a flake and more!

Has the cone been dipped in chocolate?

Some weird REAL-LIFE flavours include CURRY, BACON, OCTOPUS and CICADA (a type of insect).

It takes an average of 50 LICKS to finish a scoop of ice cream.

CAN YOU BEAT THAT?

I can finish a scoop in

_ _ _ _ LICKS.

Ever eaten ice cream, so fast you got

BRAIN FREEZE?

YES ☐ NO ☐

Ever stirred a bowl of ice cream till it turned into a liquid and then eaten it like SOUP?

☐ YES

☐ NO

In 2015, Matt Stonie ate 12 TUBS of ice cream in 36 minutes.

In 1988, two American chefs made the biggest ice cream sundae ever. It weighed 25 TONNES.

Ice cream sundae = Four elephants

HOW TICKLISH ARE YOU?

Tick or colour in the right box.

	NOT AT ALL	A BIT	A LOT	SO MUCH IT HURTS
NECK	☐	☐	☐	☐
UNDERARM	☐	☐	☐	☐

50

SIDES

BACK OF LEGS

SOLES OF FEET

MY BATHROOM

How well do you scrub up?

What colour is your toothbrush? Colour it in!

Bath or shower?

I prefer a _ _ _ _ _ _ _ _ _

I brush my teeth

_ _ _ _ _ _ _

times a day

Sponge, flannel, or just your hands? (Circle one).

Bubble bath?

☐ Yes ☐ No

Do you have your own towel?

Show us what it looks like!

Comb ☐

Hairbrush ☐

Neither ☐

Use MIRROR WRITING to complete the other page! Test it in your bathroom mirror...

52

MY BATHROOM

How well do you scrub up?

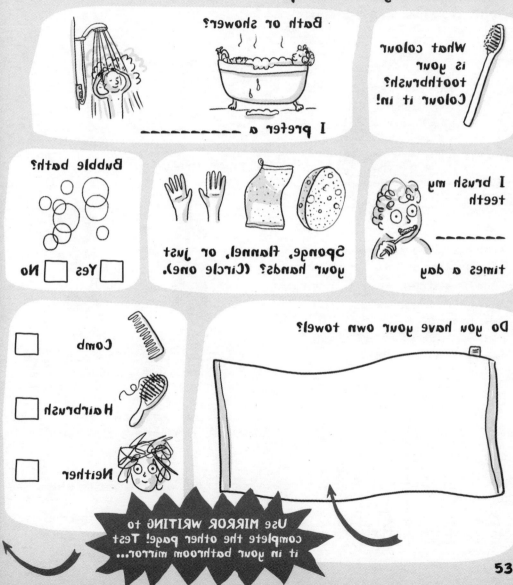

Bath or shower?

I prefer a _____

What colour is your toothbrush? Colour it in!

Bubble bath?

☐ Yes   ☐ No

Sponge, flannel, or just your hands? (Circle one.)

I brush my teeth _____ times a day

Do you have your own towel?

☐ Comb

☐ Hairbrush

☐ Neither

USE MIRROR WRITING to complete the other page! Test it in your bathroom mirror...

53

BATHROOM QUIZ

Take our quiz to see how much you know about the HISTORY of staying CLEAN.

1. Three hundred years ago, how often did most people bathe?

a. Once a week
b. Once a month
c. Twice a year

2. What did the Ancient Egyptians use to brush their teeth instead of a toothbrush?

a. A twig
b. A mummy's finger bone
c. A friend's chin

3. And what was Ancient Egyptian toothpaste made out of?

a. Cow's hooves, eggshells and myrrh
b. Camel's tail hair and mud from the River Nile
c. Mashed potato and sand

4. Before the invention of toilet roll, which of the following did people use to wipe their bottoms?

a. Corn on the cob
b. A sponge on a stick
c. Seashells
d. All of the above

5. In Indonesia, what were the first shampoos made out of?

a. Custard
b. Cowpats and tree bark
c. Rice seeds, water and straw

Check your answers at the bottom of the page and work out your score ...

SCORES

0-1	2-3	4-5
A washout!	Scrubbing up well	A clean sweep!

Answers: 1c Twice a year. Having a bath was seen (incorrectly) as spreading disease. 2a A twig. (Ouch!) 3a Cow's hooves, eggshells and myrrh. 4d All of the above! In America in the 1700s, a corncob was hung next to the toilet. In colder parts of America, mussel shells were used. Ancient Romans using public toilets all shared a sponge on a stick. 5c Rice seeds, water and straw.

TWIST IN THE TAIL

If you had a tail, which kind would it be?
Test them out on the children over there...

 **DOG**

Good for
wagging when
you're happy.

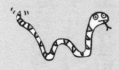 **RATTLESNAKE**

Rattle it to
warn people
off. Handy
if you're in a
band too.

STEGASAURUS

Whack any
predators
with spikes!

 MONKEY

Use it to
dangle from
branches.

 **LIZARD**

If someone
grabs it, it
comes off and
a new one
grows back.

Can you think of other cool animal tails?

Give them your dream tails

SLIPPERY SLOPE

Have you tried all the different ways of going down a slide? Which is your favourite?

Sitting up

Lying down

Head first

With a friend

Feet first

Or draw your own

The best slide ever is at:

Design your ideal playground here. We've suggested some equipment below.

Slide   Swings   Roundabout   Climbing frame   Rope bridge   Tyre swing

Climbing wall   Trampoline   Helter-skelter   Monkey bars   See-saw   Or combine these to make EVEN MORE AWESOME EQUIPMENT!

MY DAD

(Or cross out 'Dad' and put Grandad, brother or whoever you like!)

Name: _ _ _ _ _ _ _ _ _ _ _

Date of birth: _ _ _ _ _ _ _

Hair colour: _ _ _ _ _ _ _

Eye colour: _ _ _ _ _ _ _

Draw a picture of him

Draw his favourite sport here

Draw his favourite food here

What's his favourite film?

HOW HAIRY IS YOUR DAD?

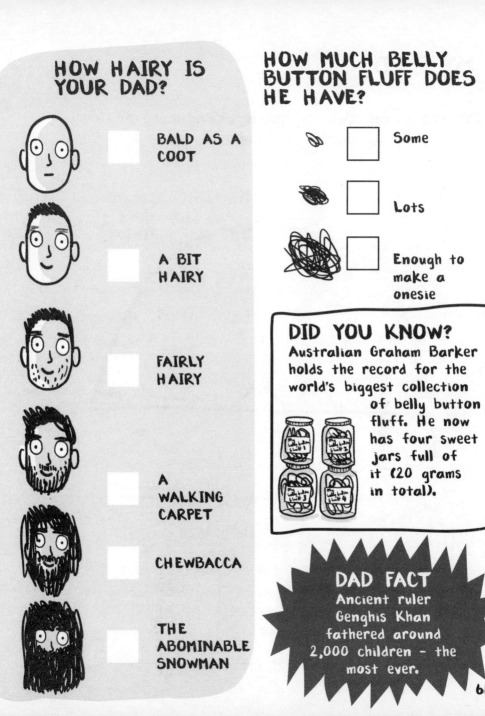

☐ BALD AS A COOT

☐ A BIT HAIRY

☐ FAIRLY HAIRY

☐ A WALKING CARPET

☐ CHEWBACCA

☐ THE ABOMINABLE SNOWMAN

HOW MUCH BELLY BUTTON FLUFF DOES HE HAVE?

☐ Some

☐ Lots

☐ Enough to make a onesie

DID YOU KNOW?
Australian Graham Barker holds the record for the world's biggest collection of belly button fluff. He now has four sweet jars full of it (20 grams in total).

DAD FACT
Ancient ruler Genghis Khan fathered around 2,000 children – the most ever.

DAD JOKES

Draw a needle on the joke-o-meter to show
how bad your Dad's jokes are.

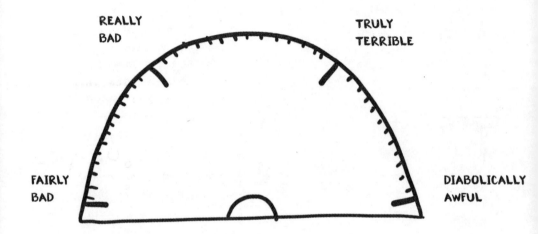

REALLY
BAD

TRULY
TERRIBLE

FAIRLY
BAD

DIABOLICALLY
AWFUL

Write your Dad's worst joke ever
here:

There are some contenders over there

Q: What do you say to three holes in the ground?
A: Well, well, well.

Two cannibals were eating a clown. One turned to the other and said: 'Does this taste funny to you?'

Me: Dad, make me a sandwich.
Dad: Abracadabra! You're a sandwich.

Two goldfish are in a tank. One turns to the other and says: 'Do you know how to drive this thing?'

Q: Why can't you hear a pterodactyl going to the toilet?
A: Because the P is silent.

BIG DADDY?

Is your Dad taller or shorter than these famous people?

200cm

150cm

50cm

0cm

Danny De Vito (actor) 152 cm

Winston Churchill 167 cm

Robert Downey Jr (Iron Man) 174 cm

Draw your Dad here!

Other tall celebrities include Liam Neeson (193 cm) – he plays Qui-Gon Jinn in 'Star Wars: Episode I' and Christopher Lee (196 cm) – Saruman in 'Lord of the Rings'.

Your Dad's height: _____ cm

Johnny Depp
(Captain Jack
Sparrow)
178 cm

King
Tutankhamun
(Egyptian
Pharaoh) 180 cm

Elvis Presley
(singer)
182 cm

Andy Murray
(tennis player)
190 cm

My Dad is about the same size as

_____

DAD DANCING

Tick the ones that your Dad does - or add you own!

 The Twist

Hips wriggling and legs clamped like he's trying to hold in a wee.

The Shuffle

Stepping from side to side like he's waiting for a bus.

 The Head Bob

Head jerks backwards and forwards. Nothing else moves.

The King of Disco

Could easily take someone's eye out.

The Rock God

Frowns like a gorilla and plays a pretend guitar.

The Total Freakout

Flings arms and legs around like he's being electrocuted.

The longest dance ever was actually performed by a MUM not a dad. In 2010, Kalamandalan Hemalatha danced non-stop for over 123 hours (more than five days).

Draw your dad dance moves here!

TEST YOUR DAD

Is your Dad a pub quiz champ?
See how he does in our tricky Dad-themed test.

1. Which is the only kind of animal where the male gives birth?

2. When was the first Father's Day? 1910, 1930 or 1950?

3. Why don't orb-weaver spiders ever meet their dads?

4. Ramajit Raghav claims to be the world's oldest dad. How old was he when his second son was born in 2012?

5. Apart from being children's writers, what do Lewis Carroll, J.M. Barrie, C.S. Lewis and Dr Seuss have in common?

6. What is the most common Father's Day gift?

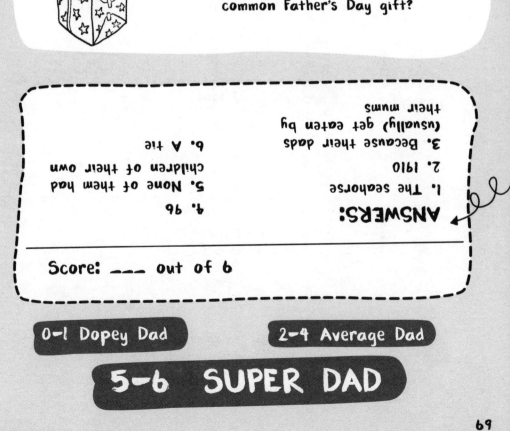

ANSWERS:

1. The seahorse

2. 1910

3. Because their dads (usually) get eaten by their mums

4. 96

5. None of them had children of their own

6. A tie

Score: ___ out of 6

0-1 Dopey Dad

2-4 Average Dad

5-6 SUPER DAD

ANIMAL MAGIC

Colour in any animals you really like, circle any animals you quite like, cross out any you don't like!

Draw any other animals you like (or don't like) here.

SCARY STUFF

Everybody's scared of something. Colour in or shade the scary-o-meter showing how scared you are of each thing.

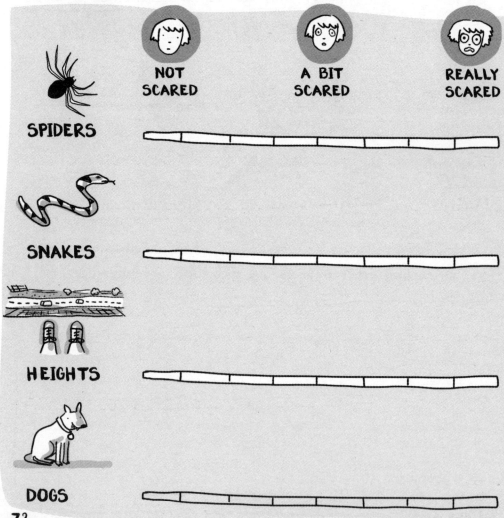

NOT SCARED   A BIT SCARED   REALLY SCARED

SPIDERS

SNAKES

HEIGHTS

DOGS

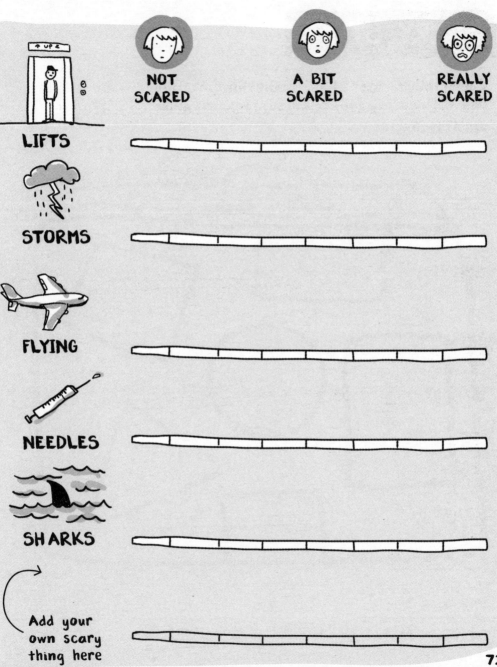

NOT SCARED

A BIT SCARED

REALLY SCARED

LIFTS

STORMS

FLYING

NEEDLES

SHARKS

Add your own scary thing here

73

GOING PLACES

Which countries have you been to?
Draw their flags or write their names
on this suitcase.

Add more labels if you need to.

My best holiday

ever was in

The other people on the

holiday were ------------.

I went for ------------

days.

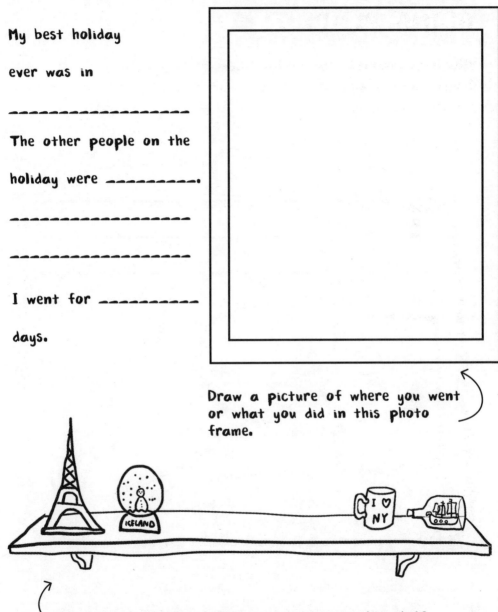

Draw a picture of where you went
or what you did in this photo
frame.

ICELAND

I ♡ NY

Draw some of your holiday souvenirs on this shelf

DREAM HOLIDAY

Which countries or places would you like to visit in the future?

Write your top 3 here:

1. _____

2. _____

3. _____

And what would you spend your time doing? Circle your top choices.

Lying on the beach

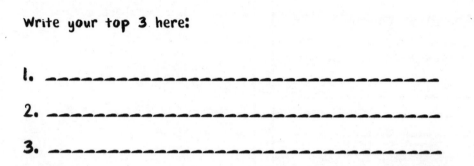
Sightseeing

Doing activities

Watching wildlife

Going on theme park rides

Skiing

Swimming

Sleeping

Need some ideas about where to go? Here are some of the most visited places in the world:

1 person = 1 million visitors

1. Niagara Falls, US/Canada — 22.5 million visitors a year

2. Disneyworld, Orlando, US — 17.5 million visitors a year

3. Forbidden City, Beijing, China — 15.3 million visitors a year

4. Notre Dame Cathedral, Paris, France — 13.7 million visitors

5. Sydney Opera House, Sydney, Australia — 8.2 million visitors a year

The most visited place in the UK is the British Museum with 6.7 million visitors a year.

Want to go to one of these places? Draw yourself in the queue!

TOP TRAVELLERS

Who's travelled the most?

 The person who has travelled the most is thought to be Fred Finn. In the course of his life, he travelled more than 15 million miles.

 That's like flying to the Moon and back over 30 times.

By the age of **37**, Gunnar Garfors had visited every single country in the world (in 2008).

He also visited these 19 countries in one day.

- ☑ Greece
- ☑ Bulgaria
- ☑ Kosovo
- ☑ Macedonia
- ☑ Serbia
- ☑ Bosnia-Herzegovina
- ☑ Croatia
- ☑ Slovenia
- ☑ Hungary
- ☑ Czech Republic
- ☑ Slovakia
- ☑ Austria
- ☑ Germany
- ☑ The Netherlands
- ☑ Belgium
- ☑ Luxembourg
- ☑ France
- ☑ Switzerland
- ☑ Liechtenstein

FLYING THE FLAG

Hurrah! You've just been declared President of Your Room. Design a flag for it here.

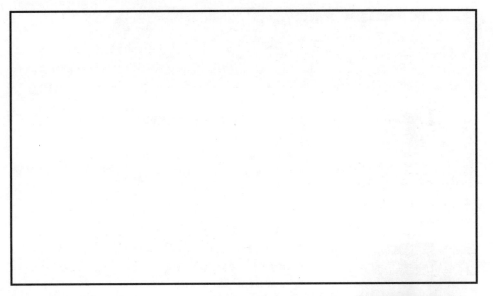

Nepal's flag is the only one that doesn't have four sides.

The Benin Empire used to have this flag: a man chopping off his enemy's head.

Bhutan

Wales

Two countries have dragons on their flags. We can't decide which is coolest. Can you?

UNUSUAL DESTINATIONS

Give each of these **REAL LIFE** tourist attractions a strangeness score from 1 to **5**.

1 = not that strange   4 = very odd
2 = a bit weird   5 = totally loopy
3 = pretty freaky

STRANGENESS SCORE

1. KARNI MATI TEMPLE, INDIA – this temple is home to about 20,000 rats. Local legends say that rats are a holy animal.

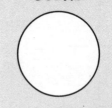

We're chilling out!

2. ICE HOTEL, SWEDEN – almost everything in this hotel is made of ice: the walls, the beds, even the glasses in the restaurant. Luckily the blankets are still woollen though.

3. BUBBLEGUM ALLEY, USA – a 21-metre-long alleyway with millions of bits of old bubblegum stuck to the walls.

4. CARHENGE, USA
– it's like Stonehenge in England, but made out of cars.

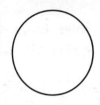

There's no place like gnome!

5. GNOME RESERVE, UK
– you'll find over 1,000 garden gnomes living freely in this huge flower garden. Visitors are encouraged to wear a pointy gnome hat.

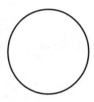

6. THE COCKROACH MUSEUM, USA
– this museum features hundreds of cockroaches dressed as celebrities and historical figures.

7. SEWER MUSEUM, PARIS
– fancy looking at rivers of poo? Then have a wee look at the sewer museum.

PACK YOUR BAGS

Circle anything you'd like to take
with you on holiday. Or draw them
inside the suitcase.

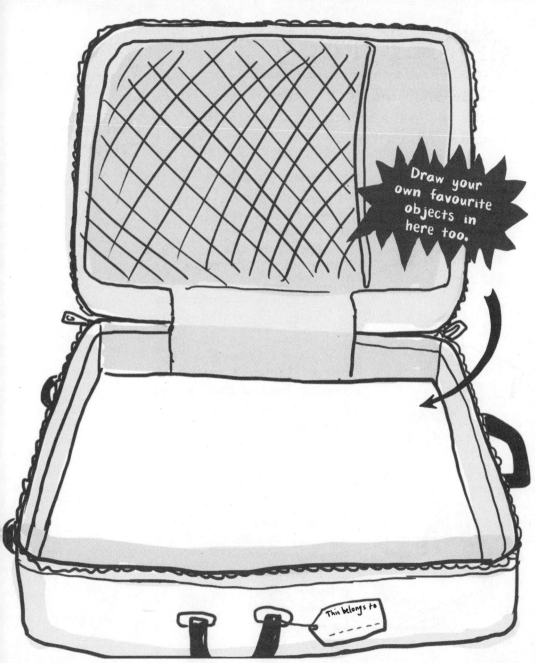

TRAVEL QUIZ

The answer to all of these questions is a SHAPE.

Draw the right shape here ↓

 1. There's an area of the Atlantic Ocean famous for ships mysteriously disappearing. It's known as the Bermuda _____.

 2. Nelson's Column is one of London's most famous landmarks. You can find it in Trafalgar _____.

 3. The Arctic _____ passes through eight different countries, including Russia, Greenland and Canada.

4. The headquarters of the U.S. Department of Defense is known as the _ _ _ _ _ _ _ _.

5. One of the most famous cricket grounds in the UK can be found in Kennington, London. It is known as the _ _ _ _ _ _ _.

6. The Hope _ _ _ _ _ is the most famous jewel in the world. Said to be cursed, ten of its previous owners have met grisly deaths. It's now in an American museum.

7. The Hollywood Walk of Fame can be found in Los Angeles. Famous actors get a _ _ _ _ _ on the pavement.

4. 20 of the 25 most venomous snakes in the world live in Australia. The most venomous is the inland taipan which can produce enough venom in one bite to kill 100 people.

5. Another Australian animal is the wombat. Its poo is cube-shaped.

6. There are more kangaroos than people in Australia. Kangaroos can't walk (or jump) backwards.

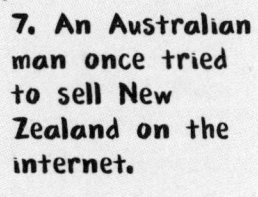

FOR SALE

7. An Australian man once tried to sell New Zealand on the internet.

Put your own Australia fact here.

AWESOME AUSTRALIA

Here are some top facts about Down Under.

1. It's over twice the size of India and 32 times bigger than the UK.

2. Its two biggest cities are Sydney and Melbourne. However these cities kept fighting over which one should be the capital. So in 1911 they created a new town - Canberra - to be the capital city.

3. Before being called Melbourne, the city had several names including Bearbrass, Bearberp and Batmania!

MOVE IT!

Draw people on or in any of these forms of transport you've been on. You can add motion lines or exhaust fumes too!

LIKE THIS!

Did we miss any you've been on? Draw them here.

SWEET DREAMS!

Draw your favourite sweets in these sweet jars.
Write their names on the labels.

They can be chocolate bars,
sweets, chewing gum or anything
else.

Are these sweet facts
TRUE or FALSE?

Answers this way!

1. If you swallow chewing gum, it stays in your stomach for three years.

gulp

2. If you leave a tooth in a glass of Coca-Cola overnight, the tooth gets dissolved.

3. There are chocolate bars called **Plopp, Fart** and **Bum Bum.**

FART

4. Candy floss was invented by a dentist.

5. You can find up to 60 bits of dead insect in the average 100g bar of chocolate.

What's the longest you've sucked a boiled sweet for?

_ _ _ _ minutes

What's the longest you've made your Easter eggs last?

_ _ _ _ _ _ days

What's the earliest time in the day you've ever been allowed sweets or chocolate?

_ _ _ _ _ _ _ _

TRUE OR FALSE ANSWERS
1. FALSE - your stomach acid can dissolve steel, it has no problem with chewing gum.
2. FALSE - it goes a bit brown, but it's still recognisably a tooth.
3. MOSTLY TRUE - Plopp is a chocolate bar in Sweden. Fart used to be a chocolate bar in Poland. Bum Bum is actually a brand of German ice cream.
4. TRUE - it was invented by dentist William Morrison in 1897.
5. TRUE - if you're in the United States, anyway. Any more than 60 dead insect parts is ILLEGAL. Less than this is not seen as dangerous to humans.

PIECE OF CAKE

In 2011, three bakeries in Canada created a cake with **255 LAYERS**.

Using your thinnest felt tips or coloured pencils, can you make 255 layers in this slice of cake?

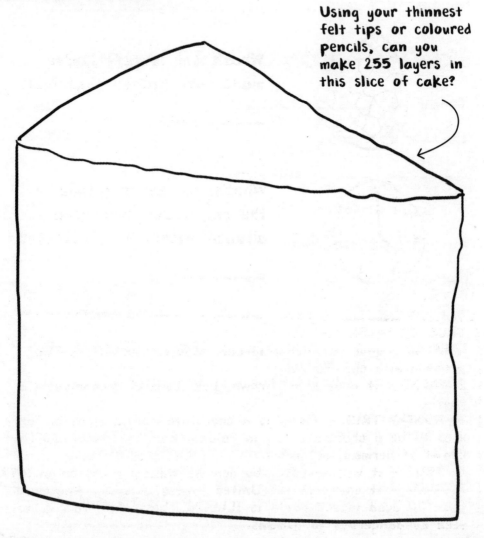

FAME!

If you were famous, what would you want to be famous for? _____

GREATEST HUMAN EVER ANNOUNCED

Today _____
(your name)
the world-famous

_____ was
(write your dream job)
officially declared the most

awesome person who has ever

lived.

Draw yourself or stick a photo here.

A recent **poll** of everyone in the world stated

that _____ was so awesome that
(write your name)
planet Earth should probably be called planet

_____ .
(write your name)
Asked to comment on their amazing qualities,

_____ said: _____
(write your name)   (what would you say?)

_____ .

94

Looking for ideas? These are some of the most famous people who have ever lived.

ISAAC NEWTON
scientist, discovered the laws of gravity

JOAN OF ARC
military leader, led the French army to several famous victories

NEIL ARMSTRONG
astronaut, first man on the Moon

WILLIAM SHAKESPEARE
playwright and poet, wrote Romeo and Juliet

LEONARDO DA VINCI
painter and inventor, painted the Mona Lisa

EMMELINE PANKHURST
activist, fought for women in the UK to get the vote

WALT DISNEY
filmmaker, creator of Mickey Mouse and more

SUPER SUPERSTITIONS

Here are some of the most common superstitions in the world. Do you believe that...

Tick one of the boxes

Yes it's true!　　No it's silly!

 Walking under a ladder is bad luck

☐ ☐

 Finding a four-leaf clover is lucky

☐ ☐

 Crossing your fingers is good luck

☐ ☐

A black cat crossing your path is bad luck

☐ ☐

 Some objects can be cursed and bring bad luck to their owners

☐ ☐

Breaking a mirror is
seven years' bad luck

☐ ☐

 A horseshoe 'collects'
good luck

☐ ☐

Friday the 13th is always
unlucky

☐ ☐

Add any
superstitions
that you believe
in here.

What about other people in your family? What do they
believe?

MAKE A SPLASH!

Love swimming? Which of these strokes can you do?

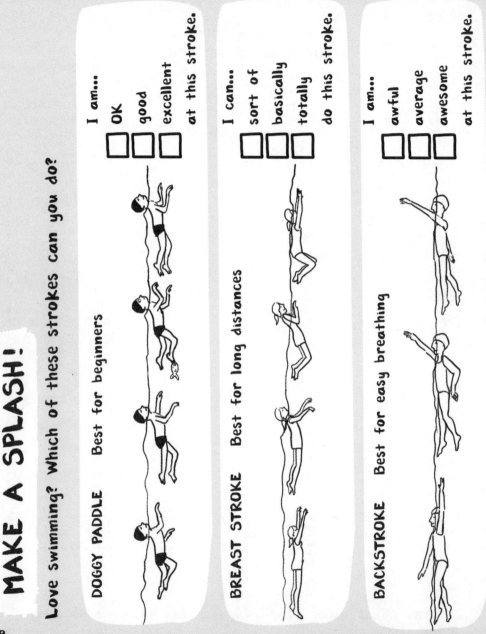

DOGGY PADDLE Best for beginners

I am...
☐ OK
☐ good
☐ excellent
at this stroke.

BREAST STROKE Best for long distances

I can...
☐ sort of
☐ basically
☐ totally
do this stroke.

BACKSTROKE Best for easy breathing

I am...
☐ awful
☐ average
☐ awesome
at this stroke.

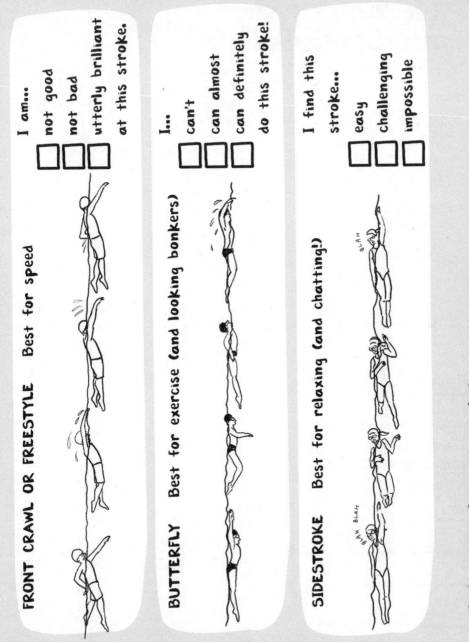

FRONT CRAWL OR FREESTYLE   Best for speed

I am...

☐ not good
☐ not bad
☐ utterly brilliant

at this stroke.

BUTTERFLY   Best for exercise (and looking bonkers)

I...

☐ can't
☐ can almost
☐ can definitely

do this stroke!

SIDESTROKE   Best for relaxing (and chatting!)

BLAH BLAH

BLAH

I find this stroke...

☐ easy
☐ challenging
☐ impossible

Which is your favourite stroke? — — — — — — — — — — —

AQUA ACROBATICS

Which of these can you do?

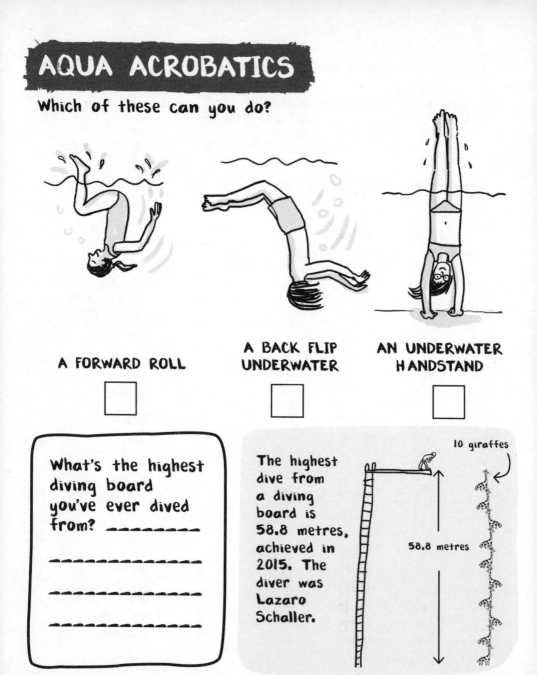

A FORWARD ROLL

A BACK FLIP UNDERWATER

AN UNDERWATER HANDSTAND

What's the highest diving board you've ever dived from? _____

The highest dive from a diving board is 58.8 metres, achieved in 2015. The diver was Lazaro Schaller.

10 giraffes

58.8 metres

What's the deepest pool you've ever been in? _____ metres

Did you jump in and touch the bottom?   Yes ☐   No ☐

The deepest swimming pool in the world is 42 metres deep. It's in Padua in Italy. It also has underwater caves!

Mariana Trench 10,994 deep

The deepest point in the ocean is the Mariana Trench. It's 10,994 metres deep. Only three people have ever visited it.

Mount Everest 8848 metres high

I'd rather   ☐ Climb Everest
             ☐ Visit the Mariana Trench

SWIMMING STATS

What are some of your personal records?

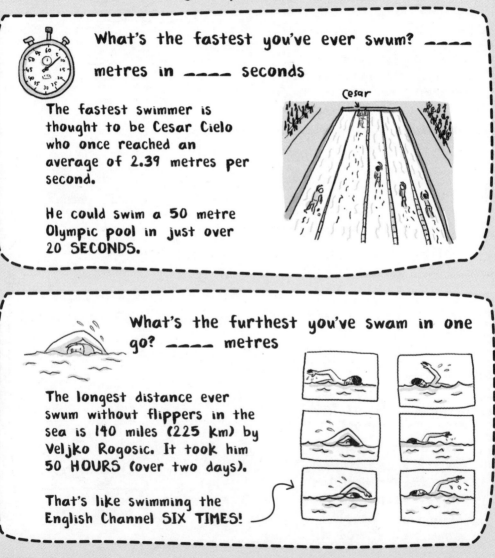

What's the fastest you've ever swum? _____ metres in _____ seconds

The fastest swimmer is thought to be Cesar Cielo who once reached an average of 2.39 metres per second.

He could swim a 50 metre Olympic pool in just over 20 SECONDS.

Cesar

What's the furthest you've swam in one go? _____ metres

The longest distance ever swum without flippers in the sea is 140 miles (225 km) by Veljko Rogosic. It took him 50 HOURS (over two days).

That's like swimming the English Channel SIX TIMES!

What or where is the longest water slide you've ever been on?

_____

The longest water slide is 610 metres long. It's in New Jersey, USA. It takes a minute and a half to get to the bottom.

The best wave **pool** I've ever been to is _____

average adult 1.8 metres

average 8 year old, 1.3 metres

The biggest wave machine in the world is said to be at the Wave Palace pool in Tenerife. The waves can reach three metres in height.

3 metre wave

THE PERFECT POOL

Describe or design your perfect pool. Will it have slides, floats and inflatables? Will anything live in the pool? How deep will the deep end be?

Some crazy ideas from real-life pools.

The water in the Library Hotel pool in Thailand is bright red!

In the aloe beads pool in China, the water has been replaced by squishy plastic balls.

The pool in the Golden Nugget hotel in Las Vegas is next to a shark tank...

In the Sanctuary Swala pool in Tanzania, you're surrounded by elephants and antelope!

The pool can be a crazy shape too.

Days Inn Hotel, Memphis

Fontainebleau Hotel, Miami

Crusoe's retreat, Fiji

Suites de Boracay, Monaco

CHOOSE YOUR SUPERPOWER

If you could only choose one, which would it be?
Circle or colour in your favourite.

Flying

Superhuman strength

Read people's minds

Super speed

SCHOOL IS COOL!

Name of your school

Which year are you in?

Who is your favourite teacher ever?

Who are your best friends?

Who's the fastest in your class?

Who's the tallest in your class?

School dinners or packed lunch?

_____

Who's the funniest in your class?

- - - - - - - - - - - - - - - - -

What's your favourite subject?

- - - - - - - - - - - - - - - -

What's your least favourite subject?

- - - - - - - - - - - - - - - - - -

What's the best fact you've ever learnt in school?

- -

- -

If you ran the world:

Which days would be school days?

MONDAY

TUESDAY

WEDNESDAY

THURSDAY

FRIDAY

SATURDAY

SUNDAY

(Circle them!)

Which days would be the weekend?

MONDAY

TUESDAY

WEDNESDAY

THURSDAY

FRIDAY

SATURDAY

SUNDAY

Which school holiday is your favourite?

☐ October half-term
☐ Summer
☐ May half-term
☐ Easter
☐ February half-term
☐ Christmas

Describe your dream school

There are some ideas over there →

TOP OF THE CLASS?

Dongzhong Primary School in China is in a cave.

In Bangladesh, over 100 schools are located on boats.

Mulleborg nursery school in Sweden is outdoors – in the middle of a forest.

Before it closed in 1995, Abo elementary school was completely underground!

KIDS RULE
At Brooklyn Free School, pupils choose what they want to study. They can also stay at home if they want. They make all the school rules too!

Home time!

PLAYGROUND FAVES

Do you ever play any of these games?

I PLAY THEM

	LOTS	SOMETIMES	RARELY	NEVER
TAG/IT	☐	☐	☐	☐
FOOTBALL	☐	☐	☐	☐
CONKERS	☐	☐	☐	☐
SKIPPING	☐	☐	☐	☐
HOPSCOTCH	☐	☐	☐	☐
MARBLES	☐	☐	☐	☐
ROCK PAPER SCISSORS	☐	☐	☐	☐
CAT'S CRADLE	☐	☐	☐	☐
HAND CLAPPING GAMES	☐	☐	☐	☐

In the 2001 World Conker Championships, Eamonn Dooley smashed 306 conkers in one hour.

YOU SMASHED IT!

In 2006, Michael and Jenna Gray played marbles for 26 hours - the longest game ever.

zzzZ

In 1974, three Americans played cat's cradle for 21 hours. They changed the cradle 21,200 times - a world record.

The oldest known game is called Senet. It's a board game, a bit like chess and is about 5,000 years old. Senet boards were found buried in Egyptian tombs.

What's your favourite playground game?

GRAFFITI!

Writing on walls usually gets you in BIG trouble. But in the pages of this book, you're free to spray away!

Ron ♡ Hermione

 PANDALISM

I hate graffiti

I woz 'ere
'Ere I woz
Woz I 'ere?
I think I woz

If you're reading this, you're about to fall over.

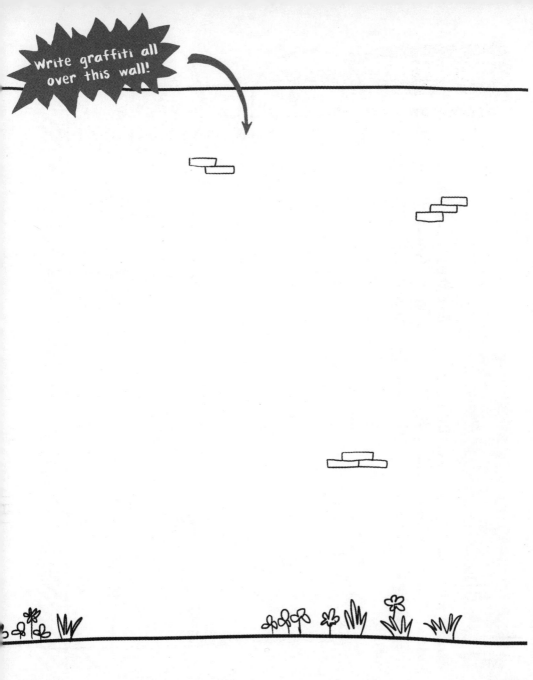

GET ON THE CASE!

Pencil cases are awesome. Draw your pencil case in the box below. Then, if you have any of the objects round the outside, draw a line connecting it to your pencil case. Or draw it inside!

Like this

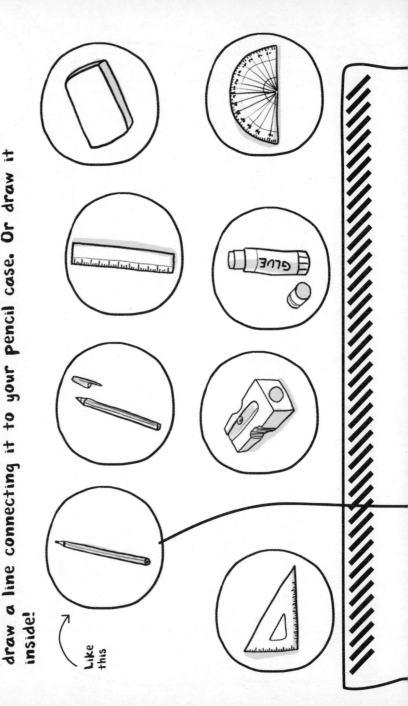

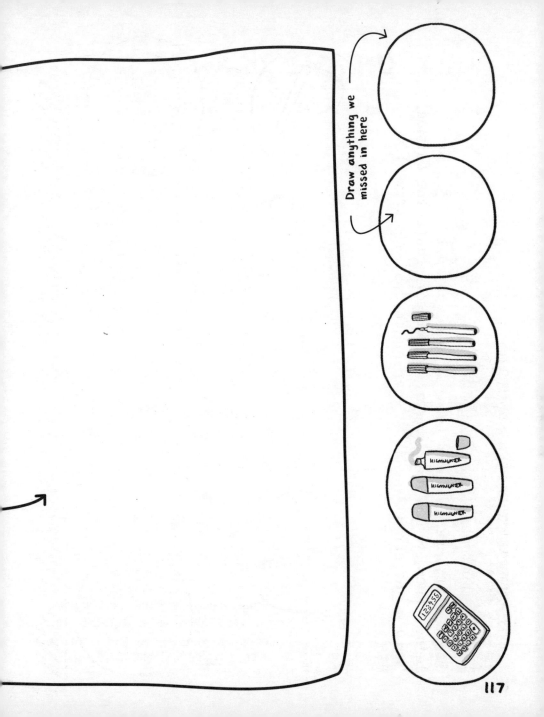

Draw anything we missed in here

117

QUICK ON THE DRAW

Some people must have massive pencil cases...

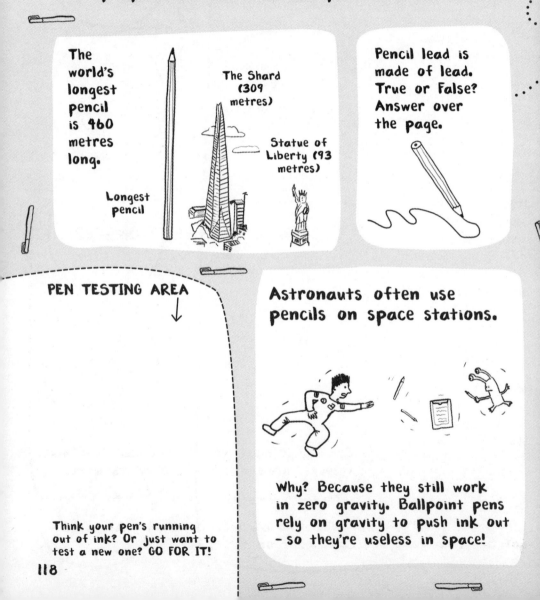

The world's longest pencil is 460 metres long.

The Shard (309 metres)

Statue of Liberty (93 metres)

Longest pencil

Pencil lead is made of lead. True or False? Answer over the page.

PEN TESTING AREA
↓

Think your pen's running out of ink? Or just want to test a new one? GO FOR IT!

Astronauts often use pencils on space stations.

Why? Because they still work in zero gravity. Ballpoint pens rely on gravity to push ink out – so they're useless in space!

The average ballpoint pen can write a line 3 kilometres long before it runs out of ink. It could draw a line around Wembley Stadium... 3 times.

Before rubbers were invented, people used a rolled-up piece of white bread to rub out pencil marks. Try it!

Rubbers aren't usually made from rubber. Most are made from artificial material such as vinyl.

DRAW A SCRIBBLE MONSTER

Draw your most insane scribble. Then give it eyes, arms and legs. Write its name.

LIFE'S BIG MYSTERIES... Where do all the lost pens go? See how many you can count on this page...

Answer:
_ _ _ _ pens

OLD NEWS

Do you know your grandparents? And your great-grandparents?

Who's the oldest person in your family?

_____

How old are they?

What's the earliest thing they remember?

_____

_____

_____

_____

The oldest person who ever lived is Jeanne Calment. A Frenchwoman, she was born in 1875 and lived until 1997, reaching **122** years of age.

WHAT DO YOU CALL YOUR GRANDPARENTS?

Circle the right names or write your own..

Nan   Nanny   Gran   Granny

Grandma   Grandpa   Grandad

Gramps   Pops   Nona   Yaya

Babushka

FALSE. It's actually a mixture of graphite and clay. Which is just as well, as lead is poisonous!

Draw your family tree here.

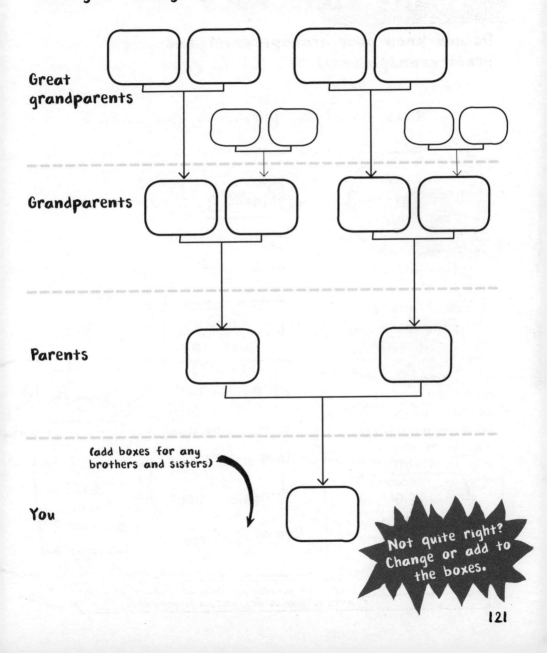

Great grandparents

Grandparents

Parents

(add boxes for any brothers and sisters)

You

Not quite right? Change or add to the boxes.

ANCIENT LANGUAGES

Do your grandparents have any favourite phrases?
Award yourself 10 POINTS if they've ever said any
of the things below.

A bonus 20 points for:

Ooh haven't you grown?

A bonus 30 points for:

Has anyone seen my glasses?

(While their glasses are balanced on their head.)

YOUR SCORE:

0-50 points
Your grandparents are pretty unusual

60-90 points
Your grandparents are fairly average

Over 90 points
You've got TEXTBOOK grandparents

DID YOU KNOW?

There's a kind of jellyfish called Turritopsis dohrnii that doesn't die (unless it's eaten or gets sick).

Once it gets old, it turns back into an adult and then a baby. Then it starts its life all over again.

WOULD YOU RATHER...?

Draw a circle around your choice.

It was
Halloween
every day   **OR**   Easter
every day

It was
your
birthday
every day   **OR**   Christmas
every day

Be able to
fly really
slowly   **OR**   Run really
fast

Own a
T-Rex   **OR**   Be a
T-Rex

Have to eat your favourite meal every day OR Never eat it again

Talk to animals OR Speak every language in the world

Time travel to the past OR Time travel to the future

Have a head the size of a ping pong ball OR A head the size of a beach ball

Always have to tell the truth OR Always have to lie

Make up your own tricky question.

I DON'T BELIEVE IT!

There's no proof that any of these creatures exist – but do you believe in them anyway?

	MADE UP	REAL	REAL AND I'VE SEEN ONE!
Ghosts	☐	☐	☐
Witches	☐	☐	☐
Vampires	☐	☐	☐
Werewolves	☐	☐	☐
Zombies	☐	☐	☐
Trolls	☐	☐	☐
The Loch Ness Monster	☐	☐	☐
The Yeti or Abominable Snowman	☐	☐	☐

Which is your favourite kind of monster? _____

MAKE YOUR OWN HAUNTED HOUSE

Cut the doors and windows out of this haunted house. Turn over the page to see where to cut.

Draw the monsters that live in it on page 129.

The backs of the windows could have spooky shapes on.
Why not draw some? Cut along the dotted lines only:

Draw your favourite monsters in those boxes, so that it looks like they are 'hiding' in the house!

The first mention of the Loch Ness monster is in a book written in 565 AD. That makes Nessie almost 1,500 years old!

Or a zombie zone?

Will it be a vampire venue?

DID YOU KNOW? Over half (52%) of people in the UK believe in ghosts.

Or a monstrous mixture?

HAPPY HALLOWEEN

It's the creepiest night of the year...

10 million pumpkins are grown in the UK every year...

= 1 million pumpkins

Draw faces on the pumpkins!

...only half a million are eaten. The others (9 ½ million) are carved into Halloween lanterns.

The biggest pumpkin ever grown weighed just over a TONNE!

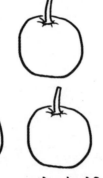

=

THAT'S THE SAME WEIGHT AS A CAR!

TRICK OR TREAT CHECKLIST

Tick them →

☐ CREEPY COSTUME

☐ MAP OF THE LOCAL AREA

☐ LARGE BAG FOR COLLECTING SWEETS

☐ GOOD MANNERS
(Grown-ups like polite kids. Weird, isn't it?)

DID YOU KNOW?
The loudest scream EVER was 129 decibels (or dB).

Motorbike = 100 dB

Rock concert = 115 dB

Pneumatic drill = 125 dB

LOUDEST SCREAM EVER = 129 dB

The screamer was Jill Dawson of the UK.

HIDE YOUR STASH!
9 out of 10 parents admit to raiding their kids' trick or treat sweets.

What's the scariest book you've ever read?

What's the scariest film you've ever seen?

CRACKING CHRISTMAS

What's the best Christmas present you've ever had?

BEST

WORST

And what's the worst present?

Where's your favourite place to be at Christmas?

☐ My house

☐ Grandparents' house

☐ Holiday

☐ ----------------- ← somewhere else?

What's your favourite Christmas song?

What would be on your best ever Christmas jumper? Draw it!

WRAP IT UP!

Design the best ever Christmas wrapping paper here.

Then buy a fairly SMALL present, rip the page out and wrap the present up!

CHRISTMAS CHAMPS

Check out these festive facts!

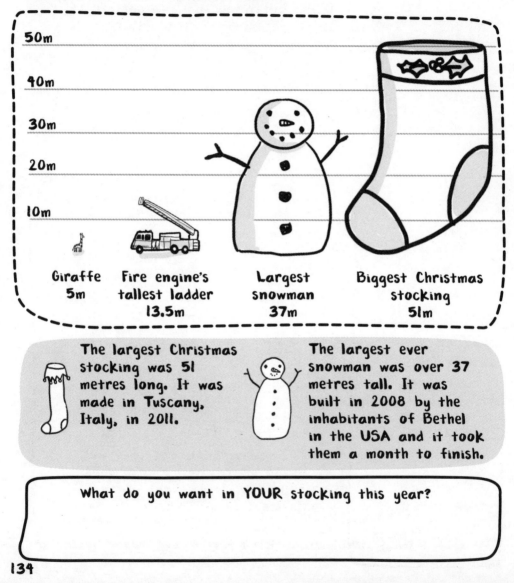

50m			
40m			
30m			
20m			
10m			

Giraffe 5m

Fire engine's tallest ladder 13.5m

Largest snowman 37m

Biggest Christmas stocking 51m

The largest Christmas stocking was 51 metres long. It was made in Tuscany, Italy, in 2011.

The largest ever snowman was over 37 metres tall. It was built in 2008 by the inhabitants of Bethel in the USA and it took them a month to finish.

What do you want in YOUR stocking this year?

FACT CHECK

THREE WISE MEN?
Wise men are mentioned in the Bible, but it doesn't say whether there were two, three or three hundred.

OH DEER!
Male reindeer shed their antlers in winter - so Rudolph and his friends wouldn't have any.

What do German children call Santa Claus?

a. Weihnachtsmann
b. Papa Noel
c. Herr HoHo

Answer over page

Statue of Liberty 93m   Big Ben 96m   Decorate it!

The tallest Christmas tree was 110.35 metres tall and weighed 300 tons. It was put up in Mexico City in 2015.

THE GREAT OUTDOORS?

Do you love the countryside? Have you...?

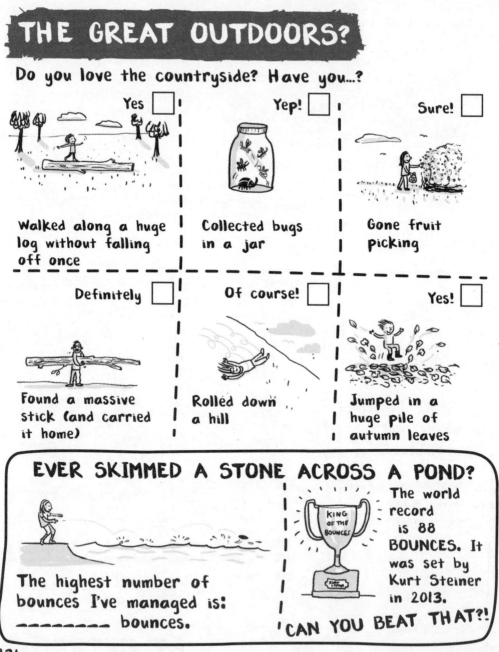

Yes ☐
Walked along a huge log without falling off once

Yep! ☐
Collected bugs in a jar

Sure! ☐
Gone fruit picking

Definitely ☐
Found a massive stick (and carried it home)

Of course! ☐
Rolled down a hill

Yes! ☐
Jumped in a huge pile of autumn leaves

EVER SKIMMED A STONE ACROSS A POND?

KING OF THE BOUNCES

The highest number of bounces I've managed is: _____ bounces.

The world record is 88 BOUNCES. It was set by Kurt Steiner in 2013.

CAN YOU BEAT THAT?!

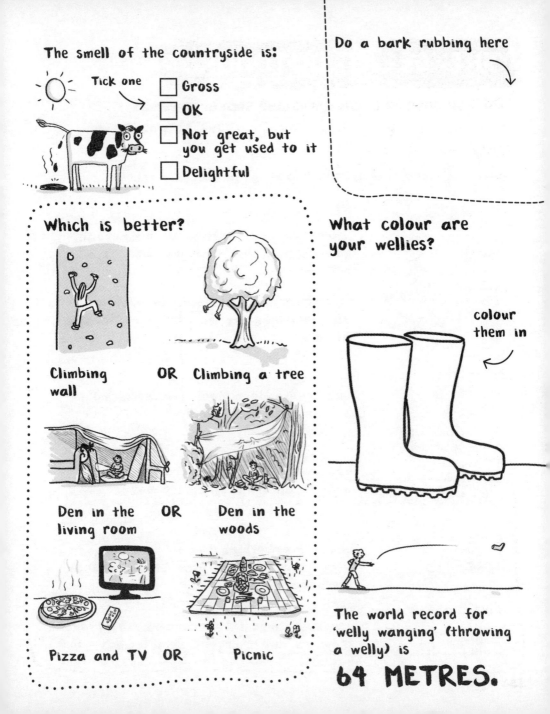

The smell of the countryside is:

Tick one

☐ Gross
☐ OK
☐ Not great, but you get used to it
☐ Delightful

Do a bark rubbing here

Which is better?

Climbing wall   OR   Climbing a tree

Den in the living room   OR   Den in the woods

Pizza and TV   OR   Picnic

What colour are your wellies?

colour them in

The world record for 'welly wanging' (throwing a welly) is

64 METRES.

CRINGE!

What are your most embarrassing moments? Give yourself points if any of these things have happened to you.

Mildly embarrassing (score **5** points for any of these)

you're playing football or basketball, you try to score and you miss by a mile

you think you're singing to yourself and then you realise everyone's looking at you

you try to do a cool gymnastic move and instead you fall over

you walk round all day with your jumper or shirt on inside out

you get something out of your bag or pencil case and all your stuff falls out everywhere

you spill some water on your skirt or trousers and everyone thinks you've wet yourself

Very embarrassing (score 10 points for any of these)

 you do a loud fart in front of the whole class

 you laugh while you're eating or drinking and stuff squirts out of your nose

 you accidentally lock yourself in the toilet and can't get out

 you realise you've had a bogey hanging from your nose all day and nobody told you

Extremely embarrassing (score 20 BONUS POINTS if you have ever...):

 accidentally called your teacher 'Mum'!

POINTS
0-20 Cool customer
30-60 A bit accident-prone
70-90 A total embarrassment!

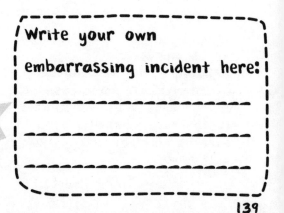

Write your own embarrassing incident here:

_____

_____

_____

SPACE VACATION

If you could visit another planet in the solar system, which would you choose? Draw an astronaut or a spacelab on your favourite planet.

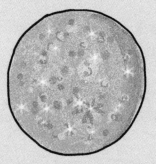

MERCURY
For every one Earth year, Mercury has over four! So you'd get FOUR times as many birthdays. There's no atmosphere though – which means the weather never changes. A bit boring?

VENUS
Venus has lots of amazingly cool volcanoes. But everything smells of rotten eggs (sulphur) and the average temperature is over 450°C. Hot enough to melt lead!

MARS

Gravity is weak here so you can jump THREE TIMES higher than on Earth. But it's freezing (~140°C) in the winter. And it gets dust storms that last for MONTHS.

JUPITER

Jupiter is giant - 1,300 times bigger than Earth. So there's LOTS to explore. But it's made of gas so you'd have problems walking on it.

SATURN

Saturn has amazing rings! Eight big ones and hundreds of small ones! Plus 60 moons! But its atmosphere is so strong, you'd get squished in seconds.

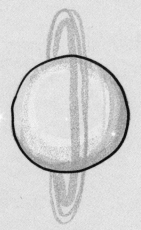

URANUS
There's lots of ice here if you feel like making a snowman. Wear oven gloves though because the ice is boiling hot!

NEPTUNE
We don't know much about Neptune so you'd be on a fantastic fact-finding mission. It would take you 10 years to get there though. How old would you be?

Or would you rather live on a moon or dwarf planet? Europa? Titan? Pluto? Tell us WHERE and WHY.

RED LETTER DAY

Five-year-old Oliver Giddings asked the Royal Mail how much it would cost to send a letter to Mars. He was given the answer: £11,602.25. That's about the cost of a family car.

X. PLORER
3rd Crater on the left
MARS

=

NO GOING BACK

Nobody has ever visited any of the other planets in the solar system.

NASA

Bye forever!

NASA is hoping to launch its first manned mission to Mars in the 2030s. This would be a ONE-WAY TRIP – with no chance of coming back.

Would you want to go on a one-way trip to Mars?
Yes ☐ No ☐

A BIT OF A STRETCH

Did you know that your spine stretches in space? Astronauts in a space station end up around 5 centimetres taller. How tall would that make you?

Height on Earth:

_____

Height in space:

_____

143

SAY WHAT?

Almost a billion people in the world speak English. And everyone says things differently.

How do you pronounce these words (circle how you say it)?

Or write it your way...
↓

Baff   Barth   Baarf   Bay-ath

choc-lit   choco-lit   chahk-lit
chawk-lit

Vitamin   Vidamin   Vyde-amin

Dogg   Dorg   Dahg   Dawg

And what is it you're reading right now?

Buuk (to rhyme with puke)
Buk (to rhyme with shook)

What do you call these things?
(Circle your choices – or write your own).

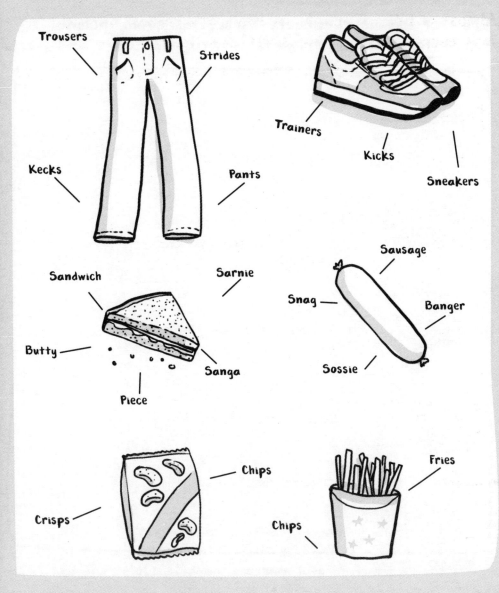

Trousers

Strides

Kecks

Pants

Trainers

Kicks

Sneakers

Sandwich

Sarnie

Butty

Sanga

Piece

Sausage

Snag

Banger

Sossie

Chips

Crisps

Fries

Chips

GO GO GADGET

Draw or list your gadgets here. This could include calculators, Xboxes, remote control dinosaurs and more.

You can include your parents' gadgets too if you like.

Which gadget could you not live without?

If you could own any gadget in the world, what would it be?

Which of your friends is MOST obsessed with gadgets? (Or is it you?)

Design a pet robot here.

PHOTO BOOTH

Take a photo of yourself pulling these faces.
Print them out and stick them here.

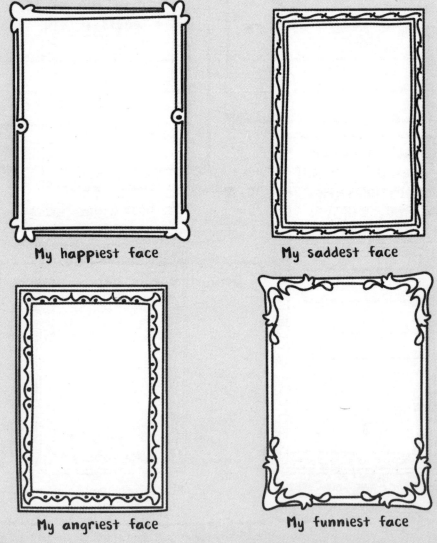

My happiest face

My saddest face

My angriest face

My funniest face

These photos are more challenging, so sketch yourself if you prefer!

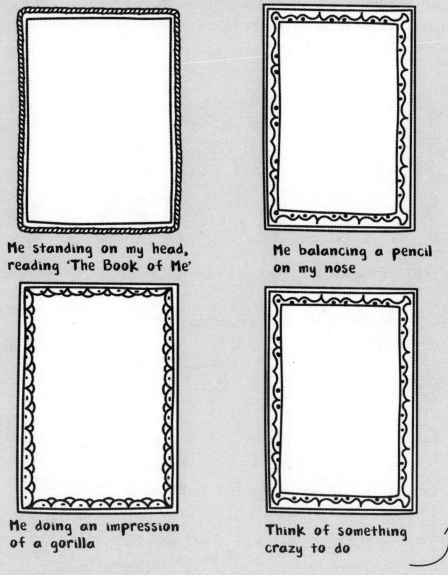

Me standing on my head, reading 'The Book of Me'

Me balancing a pencil on my nose

Me doing an impression of a gorilla

Think of something crazy to do

PARTY TIME

Time to dress up and have tons of fun!
What's your favourite thing to dress up as?

| Pirate | Superhero | Princess | Cowboy | Vampire | Or something else? |

What's your favourite face painting design?

| Tiger | Butterfly | Monster | Fairy | Spiderman | Or something else? |

What was the longest conga line ever?

Who's invited to your dream party?

> Dear ----------
>
> and ----------
>
> and ----------
>
> and ----------
>
> and ----------
>
> and ----------
>
> Please come to my party!

At your dream party, what three games would you play?

> ### GAMES LIST
>
> 1. ----------
>   ----------
> 2. ----------
>   ----------
> 3. ----------
>   ----------

some ideas

Pass the parcel

Musical statues

Musical bumps

Grandmother's footsteps

Duck duck goose

Sleeping lions

Musical chairs

Or do you know better games?

Make the best **party bag** ever! Write or draw FIVE things inside.

Sweets

Party popper

Whistle

Book

More sweets

Yo-yo

Cake

Lollipop

Stickers

Wind-up toy

Incredibly bouncy ball

Even more sweets

Use one of our suggestions or make up your own ideas!

Choose a balloon animal (or object) to make at your party:

Dog

Sword

Butterfly

Giraffe

Flower

Or draw your own?

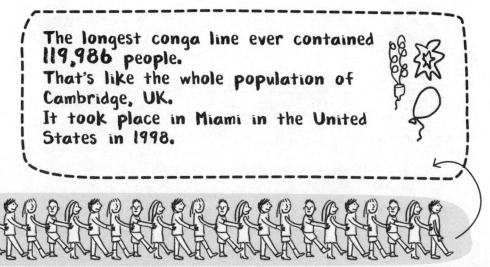

The longest conga line ever contained 119,986 people.
That's like the whole population of Cambridge, UK.
It took place in Miami in the United States in 1998.

GAME ON!

Circle any of these sports you've tried. Colour them in if you like them!

Did we miss out your favourite sport? Draw or write it here.

GO TEAM!

Do you support a football team? Draw or colour in their strip.

Home strip   Away strip

If you don't like football, just design your own cool sports kit.

Favourite football player:

- -

ODD OLYMPICS

Over its history, the Olympics has given out medals to all kinds of strange events. Here are just some of them...

Tug-of-war

Hot-air ballooning

Epic poetry

Tandem racing

Singing

Which activity would you LOVE to see as an Olympic sport?

Olympic gold medals are made out of gold.

True or False?

It's the end of the book. Time for a rest.

Design a cool pair of pyjamas here.

What's the longest you've ever kept your pyjamas on in a single day? (Not counting when you're sick).

False. They were made out of solid gold until 1912 but since then, they've been made mostly out of... SILVER!

I woke up at:

I finally took pyjamas off at:

Write the time!

What's the weirdest dream you've ever had?

What's your favourite position to sleep in?

Circle it or colour it in!

SOURCES

For The Book of Me, I found facts everywhere — in brilliant books, on wonderful websites and in nifty newspapers. Here are just some of them:

Brilliant books:

Guinness World Records (Guinness World Records, 2015)
Knowledge Encyclopedia (Dorling Kindersley, 2013)
Superhuman Encyclopaedia (Dorling Kindersley, 2014)
5000 Awesome Facts (About Everything) (National Geographic, 2012)
1227 QI Facts to Blow Your Socks Off — Kindle Edition by John Lloyd and John Mitchinson (Faber and Faber, 2012)
1339 QI Facts to Make Your Jaw Drop — Kindle Edition by John Lloyd and John Mitchinson (Faber and Faber, 2013)
Plus the QI TV show and the QI Elves on Twitter
The Horrible History and Horrible Science books.

Wonderful websites:

http://kids.britannica.com/
www.guinnessworldrecords.com
www.nationalgeographic.com/
qi.com
http://www.newscientist.com/
http://www.nasa.gov/

And, of course, Google.

Nifty newspapers:

The Guardian
The Independent
The Telegraph

For a list of all the sources I used, see: http://bit.ly/23dRlcx